LEGAL MINDS

Also by Robert L. Davis

COP OUT

For more information, visit the Web site at:

www.authorsden.com/copout

LEGAL MINDS

✦

Detecting Rogue Police Officers and Other Important Law Enforcement Issues

Robert L. Davis and
Dr. Roxanne M. Davidson

iUniverse, Inc.
New York Lincoln Shanghai

LEGAL MINDS
Detecting Rogue Police Officers and Other Important Law Enforcement Issues

iUniverse books may be ordered through booksellers or by contacting:

iUniverse
2021 Pine Lake Road, Suite 100
Lincoln, NE 68512
www.iuniverse.com
1-800-Authors (1-800-288-4677)

Because of the dynamic nature of the Internet, any Web addresses or links contained in this book may have changed since publication and may no longer be valid.

The information, ideas, and suggestions in this book are not intended to render legal advice. Before following any suggestions contained in this book, you should consult your personal attorney. Neither the author nor the publisher shall be liable or responsible for any loss or damage allegedly arising as a consequence of your use or application of any information or suggestions in this book.

ISBN: 978-0-595-48609-0 (pbk)
ISBN: 978-0-595-60703-7 (ebk)

Printed in the United States of America

For the victims of rogue law enforcement officers

Contents

About this Book

This book is a series of questions asked over several months concerning law enforcement issues asked of *Cop Out* author Robert L. Davis by everyday common citizens. The author, a former New Orleans police officer, noticed countless ordinary citizens were unaware of many law enforcement questions and issues and thought it would be helpful to collaborate with Dr. Roxanne M. Davidson, an Associate Professor of Behavioral Studies at Southern University and A&M College located in Baton Rouge, Louisiana.

Queries were taken from Mr. Davis' question and answer sessions with diverse people from all walks of life over several months. Dr. Davidson provides her professional opinion and assessment of the potential motives, reasons, and behavior patterns of the criminal.

The purpose of their collaboration is examining the innumerable crimes committed by people on humankind and tries to answer not only how certain criminals might execute specific crimes, but more importantly rationale for such unlawful acts. This book is an attempt to consider plausible and possible explanations of human behavior and in no way attempts to say *precisely* the reasons such crimes occurred with absolute certainty. Both authors are aware of the various opinions shared by masses of people in law enforcement and in academia concerning this crucial subject. Moreover, the authors strongly encourage anyone with serious law enforcement issues to seek professional counsel.

In addition, readers will discover practical comments about how to possibly avoid rogue police officers, the definition of a rogue cop, tips on certain signs of bad cops, and the reporting of such law enforcers to the proper authorities. The authors hope these guidelines could possibly save a human life or at least help one avoid bad and unfair police officers.

Acknowledgments

I would especially like to thank Dr. Davidson for taking time out of her busy schedule and accept my proposal to offer her comments in this book. I truly feel she contributes to the various subjects contained in this book immensely; not only from an academic standpoint, but from her diverse experiences as a native New Orleanian (as I am). The readers will find, as I have, her comments are insightful, honestly expressed, and most of all without bias.

∞§∞§∞§∞§∞§∞§∞§∞§∞§∞§∞§∞§∞§∞§∞§∞§∞§∞§∞

Before you read this book about how to detect a rogue police officer, I wish to let those of you who are unaware of my past know a little something about me, as well as my knowledge concerning this significant topic. I am a former New Orleans police officer who authored a book called *Cop Out*, a powerful and riveting memoir about my former life as a fugitive for over twenty years. What's remarkable is many of those years were spent in various woods, forests, and national parks in Canada and the United States. This book has been extremely well received; primarily, because I tell the truth about others and myself with unvarnished honesty.

Cop Out is about my former life as an officer—a rogue police officer. As an officer, I received many accolades and won a prestigious award. I probably was a superior and honorable officer 99.9% of my tenure. However, I committed one bad act. As a result, I'll be remembered or should I say shamed for life. Life doesn't always reward for good, but it will certainly convict one for life for bad.

In my hometown of New Orleans, many of the cops during my tenure were corrupt cops. Even today, police officers are arrested in New Orleans probably more than many cities in America. The reason ... corruption is not stagnant, it's transient. It flows like a water hydrant until closed. If allowed to exist, it will infect almost everyone in its path.

New Orleans is the home to many alleged cop rapists, suspected cop killers, and also home to Antoinette Franks, a woman deemed the first serial/spree police officer. Presently, she sits on death row in St. Gabriel, Louisiana. The city is also home to Len Davis, allegedly a police hit man. Currently, he sits on federal death row in Terre Haute, Indiana.

I've written in my book and stated in several interviews, the city's police force is toxic. My arrest and numerous officers' arrests occurred during the 70's. Cops were arrested in the 80's and 90's, and some are detained in the current year. Definitely, there are first-class cops in New Orleans, but you might never hear of them. The bad overshadows the good.

I can't go back and make things right. Countless times I've apologized to others, myself, and to God for what I did to citizens, but the hurt won't leave. I can't apologize personally to the countless people I've hurt on that insane path. I have even been threatened and warned through the grape-vine if I continue to expose rogue cops something is going to happen to me. However, one thing I can do within my power I will ... to author books and tell all to protect and inform the public about this dark and secret group—rogue police officers.

Currently, I speak to youths, groups, and schools admonishing all peo-ple about the dangers and perils of police corruption and crime. I have dedicated my life to revealing *all* the dirty secrets and unfair practices, not just of New Orleans police officers, but all rogue cops everywhere!

Robert L. Davis

Introduction

Legal Minds does not pretend to be the sole authoritative book, manual, or guide explaining the phenomenon of rogue police officers. However, *Legal Minds* may be the beginning of several potentially newly released books concerning this unique and important subject. Simply speaking, there are not many books on the market dealing with rogue cops.

Various readers might wonder what makes me an authority on this subject. Neither I nor my co-author pretends to be the only voice revealing bad cops. Nevertheless, we are certainly a voice that has attempted to tackle this complex subject.

As a trained former police officer within an undeniably major metropolitan police department, specifically the New Orleans Police Department (who financed my university courses in criminal law), I was thoroughly skilled in *all* aspects of law enforcement and applied my training in numerous veritable situations. I arrested countless individuals, investigated several crimes, and was called to probe actual burglaries, thefts, rapes, domestic issues, assaults, robberies, frauds, and other tangible incidents. Unfortunately, I experienced a rare occurrence every law enforcement officer fears the most—being involved in a shoot-out! Not many police officers in their entire careers experience such terror—not to mention exiting alive.

Moreover, I believe I'm one of the first rogue police officers that voluntarily elected to chronicle my journey. It is natural for one to hide a dreadful past. However, I expose my previous actions in order to make a difference. As a result, I hope all police officers learn from my mistakes. Please keep in mind, I am discussing bad cops, not reputable cops.

In addition, I perceive a few readers might inquire about various articles examining commonsensible laws. Well, what is simple and straightforward to one person may not be clear-cut to another. Some of my readers and supporters are merely unaware of even the most basic elements of law. They include the elderly, the uneducated or simply the uninformed. When an individual asks me a question, no matter how simple or how many times I've answered that question, I'm obligated to respond.

To those seeking technical knowledge about a law, this book will not provide that information. Dr. Davidson and I do not want to mislead any hard-core law student, attorney or anyone that we are offering a procedural manual of law.

Finally, to those who do not believe bad cops are arrested and prosecuted daily, search the internet and you will be disappointed quickly. For example, a *Washington Post* staff writer found within the Washington, D.C. area, thirty-four police officers were arrested in 2007. That's astounding! There are literally hundreds of law enforcement officers arrested every year. One is too many, especially if it's you or a loved one.

In closing, if you find *Legal Minds* helpful, do your fellow citizens a favor and share it with a person that is unfamiliar with the signs of rogue cops, or needs information regarding lie detector tests, or may be unknowledgeable about Miranda rights.

Now, let's delve into this valuable and practical tool.

1

ROGUE POLICE OFFICERS

What is a Rogue Police Officer?

Driving on our interstate highways or residential streets can be a mundane and routine event in our lives. We drive to the store, pick up our children, or simply handle our everyday chores. However, there is one thing that can ruin your day. It's an unexpected event like being pulled over by a police officer.

This article will give you some solid tips to avoid and detect rogue police officers. These remarks should be informative especially for female drivers.

What is a rogue police officer? It's the type of officer who doesn't mind violating your rights; the kind of officer that if given the opportunity, will take advantage of a lone female. It is an officer who will extort money from you to overlook a citation or an officer who will plant illegal contraband in your vehicle (although rare). In the extreme, it's an officer who will shoot you (although uncommon) under certain circumstances to receive accolades, press, promotions, and upgrades to his vocation. Do you get the picture? In other words, a rogue officer is a dangerous person with a badge.

Below are five tips that could probably alert you to a rogue police officer:

a. A rogue cop will speak excessively about how the citation he's about to give you is extremely expensive. He will chatter about how it might increase your insurance rates, etc.

b. A rogue officer will order you out of your vehicle, but refuse to let you observe his search. He may attempt to plant an illegal item inside your vehicle.

c. A rogue police officer will demand you move your vehicle to a remote or dark location. This could be a side street, alley, etc.

d. A rogue officer speaks with such authority it seems as if the highway or street you're driving on is owned by him personally. Words like my town, my street, or my city comes to mind.

e. After he pulls you over (females beware), he insists you get out the car, looks you up and down, asks casually if you are married, or asks questions having nothing to do with the infraction at hand. In addition, after viewing the address on your driver's license, he may ask what part of town your street is located within the city.

As you all know, I was formerly a rogue police officer. Moreover, many of you recognize I feel my mission in life now is to reveal *all* rogue and unjust police officers.

In 1979, while a police officer, I would have won the top award for unfairness. However, I repented. Through my repentance, I must expose, expose, expose! Honorable officers should not have a problem with me, right? Only the bad ones!

Remember to drive safe, obey the laws, and arrive home safely.

Special: Rogue or Bad Cops—What Makes Them Who They Are?

Earlier this evening, I was speaking with author Stephen K. Peach (*Friendly Fire? The Good, the Bad, and the Corrupt*) another revealer of rogue cops in California, an ex-swat officer (glad I'm not alone). We were discussing reasons we have taken on this dangerous mission to expose rogue cops and their superiors. The answer is quite simple: A strong sense of duty to correct that which is simply wrong. Stephen was not rogue; I was, but the end results are the same. He hated rogue cops and I hated myself.

What is it that causes a police officer to violate his oath? What causes an officer to defy common decency or to travel the same road as a common criminal? What might cause an officer to rape, kill, unlawfully cite or abuse his fellow humans? Surely you will say power or some other connected issue, but the main reason might surprise you—low self esteem and worth! That's mainly the reason he joined the force (yes, me too). Most of these officers had no solid family structure or values. In many cases no parents, a lack of a parent or no loving parents. Also, they were never held accountable for their actions and in some cases, were commended either verbally or silently when doing wrong.

Then, the problem appeared when they reached the age to become an officer. They searched for a vocation or job that would let them compensate. They desired to fit a mode of respectability and honor, so some chose to become police officers or attached themselves to any law enforcement agencies (yes, the Federal Bureau of Investigation, sheriffs, state police, or even some security guards are rogue).

I know this is a deep subject I'm examining, but trust me, if you or your children ever run into these people, your life will never be the same. Their unfair tactics and procedures will cause a good citizen to resent law enforcement and the law in general.

If you've read my book *Cop Out*, you will see clearly how I was raised and where my life was heading. I was reared by my grandmother, a loving lady who did the best she could with nine siblings; except she was too old, too frail, and too sickly to fully perform the task.

There is a simple reason parents were meant to have children while they are young. The parents should be vibrant, active, healthy, and youthful to keep up with a younger version of themselves. Sure, some children do well as adults without a stable home or family, but that's the exception, not the rule. Usually, they had some other role model or some guideline to set the example.

So in closing, in my humble opinion, fathers, love your children and give them the assurances they need. Mothers, embrace your children and never forget to say these three words: *I love you!*

Finally, to all rogue cops, it's never too late to change. Change now or you will pay the price later. I certainly did!

COMMENTS FROM DR. DAVIDSON

A rogue law enforcement official is a burden to society. Whether this person becomes rogue due to low self-esteem or power and authority issues, the pain inflicted upon individuals, families, or communities is the same.

Low self-esteem is usually the result of harsh words an individual has heard from a loved one or close associate causing this person's sense of worth to decline. Power and authority issues may stem from a lack of control leading to compensation in other life skill areas. Naturally, one's vocation may convey personal desires to control others to compensate for low self-efficacy.

While this may be the case for the rogue law enforcement official, there may be other self-identity issues at hand. For example, lack of parental guidance or support from extended family and friends, inappropriate role models, lack of trust, desire for supremacy, root of bitterness, lack of spiritual development, and the basic need for love might add to the demise of one's soul. These are just a few instances that make a person rogue. A professional mental health provider could assist with cognitive development and behavioral changes for those suffering from these issues.

Rogue Police Officers—What To Do!

Many people buy life, home, and disability insurance. Yet, it astounds me how many people don't purchase legal insurance. What do I mean? I'm talking about while driving your vehicle (or your children driving your vehicle). You don't have the slightest knowledge about how to deal with a police officer if you're stopped. But if arrested, you will view this experience as seriously as any other life threatening event.

First, advise your children that if stopped by the police, pay attention. Tell them not to argue with the police, immediately take the ticket, and leave. Also, inform them if arrested by an officer, notify the officer they wish to speak with an attorney or their parents. Really alert them accordingly. Moreover, don't permit your children to drive after 10:00 p.m., especially on weekends. Many marginally rogue police officers become bolder late at night.

I was a rogue officer. I know unfair police tactics and the times they are most likely to strike.

Drive safe, obey the laws, and practice your encounters with the police *before* you meet them.

Filing Complaints Against Rogue Officers

This article will deal with a very significant question. Why should you make a complaint against a rogue police officer?

This question will only become important if you or a member of your family have been violated. Most people don't care what happens to others unless it hits home. When it does, then we try our best to bring the police officer and the department down to its knees.

Here's a suggestion. Pretend a member of your family was raped, murdered or robbed. Envision it's your daughter who was assaulted in the vilest way while driving home from soccer practice. Imagine your only son was punched in the face for no reason at all while driving home from school. Picture that while driving to your local market, you were asked to do something with a perfect stranger that you only perform with your husband or wife. Imagine your beautiful and lovely grandchildren were sodomized, raped, robbed and killed by a rogue cop.

Folks, this is an incredibly dangerous world we live in. Just when you become relaxed and feel secure in your life, a dagger goes through your heart. An encounter with a bad cop will feel this way and change your life.

When *any* law enforcer, whether an FBI agent or a forest game warden violates your civil rights, complain.

Every law enforcement agency in America has an Internal Affairs Division to deal with complaints by citizens against law officers. Don't hesitate. This same officer will violate another citizen shortly. Do your duty and report this person.

Rogue police officers are worse than common criminals. They pretend to be honorable to citizens, but deep inside they are two-bit criminals.

The badge is nothing in itself; it's what the badge stands for—honor and loyalty to a people that trust in your oath to perform with dignity in the community. I violated that trust many years ago. But I intend with every bone in my body to regain the trust and dignity of my past profession so I may one day be able to live with myself. Report all violators, period!

Police Brutality

Kevin P. asked, "What is police brutality?" I knew it would only be a matter of time before this question would arise. Well, I'm ready.

Police brutality is more than just an officer hitting or beating you. It's when a police officer has abused his powers and violated your civil rights. Usually, it does take the form of him actually hitting you in some fashion. These are rogue cops. Even the police department doesn't care for these officers.

Actually, rogue cops are thugs with a badge. They don't care about males, females, your daughters or sons, grandchildren, no one! The only thing they care about is pats on the back from other rogue cops and their superiors, accolades from the department, promotions, etc. These are the officers I'm trying to expose. Why? I was once this type of person. Had an award been given for rogue cop of the year, I would have won at least three years in a row.

I despise this person, like I hated myself. They not only ruin your life, but their family's life as well. They are the officers you hear about on television arrested for robberies, rapes, and in some cases, murders. They are vile, insane, and inhuman. A rogue officer is guided by his own brand of justice: warped and deformed. He doesn't care about the universal motto of all departments, which is to protect and serve. His slogan is to seize and serve *his* needs.

A rogue cop is an officer that slipped through the review processes, and eventually does much harm before the department knows what hit them. He gives all officers an invalid and warped reality of a good officer. Typically, he doesn't care about his own family members. He has no sense of justice.

I know this will cause a few of you to be scared; you should be. Long ago, I and this rogue officer could wreck havoc with your life for years to come. If you think it's not true, then wait until you run across one. You'll see.

Arm yourself now. Learn about rogue cops. Many of them loathe me. Some were good friends that asked me not to share these words. However, the true repentance of a man or woman is to do what's right, not to do what's non-controversial.

Drive carefully, stay alert, obey the laws, and arrive home safely to your family.

Take care, your brother.

COMMENTS FROM DR. DAVIDSON

Brutality in any form is evil. However, when occurring by those in positions of authority and trust, it stings with pain. Cruelty toward persons who are powerless and fearful may be a sign of domination and control.

Unresolved anger may cause law enforcement officials to become vicious human beings. Their authoritative position in the community may create a sense of empowerment, particularly for the person suffering from internal anguish. Perhaps, long working hours or lack of adequate rest contributed to the use of physical force. Yet, there is no excuse to pummel *any* citizen.

One of the best interventions for rough treatment of others is anger management and/or stress management techniques performed under the supervision of a mental health provider. These techniques provide tools for appropriate resolution of intense situations.

When Can the Police Use Physical Force?

Denise L. asked, "Under what circumstances can the police use deadly force or any force?" I've been asked this question repeatedly over the last few weeks and I'm ready to address this.

First, a police officer cannot indiscriminately touch you without a lawful reason, and I mean just that, a *lawful* reason. His touching you must be written in the annals of his state's law. If not, he can (through your proper complaint) be terminated and even sued for violation of your civil rights as well as criminally charged. All this means is no one can improperly touch you without cause.

As for deadly force, his decision to reach this point is so serious he could actually be placed in a state prison with other inmates. This is considered so severe that much of a police officer's training in the academy now centers on this subject.

Examples that he might use deadly force: You are in possession of a deadly weapon and the officer truly feels his life is in danger or he feels *great* bodily harm. In other words, the person in question might use the weapon. Even if you never intended to use the weapon is not relevant. His using deadly force is a law based on what a normal person would feel if presented with these circumstances. This also includes such things as attempting to run over an officer with your automobile or other motorized vehicle.

Examples not using deadly force: The officer knows you have no intention to harm him in any way or the means to harm him. A genuine example would be shooting or hitting a handcuffed prisoner. Another instance involves shooting or hitting a driver for a traffic violation or a simple pedestrian stop. Moreover, hitting or shooting an individual under any circumstances that the officer knows or should have known there is no threat.

The job of a police officer is extremely dangerous. One must not forget that he is a human being also, but unfairly, he must *not* make any serious mistakes that can cause a loss of life. I say unfairly because we all know mistakes in any endeavor will happen. That's part of the job.

Recently, one reader sent me correspondence stating I should not defend a cop under any circumstances. Well, when I started writing these articles and even writing my book, I never claimed I would not support the police if they are justified. In fact, I feel a need to stand up for an honorable police officer just like anyone else. However, I also stated I would not defend a rogue officer.

I was once a rogue officer. As a result, I despise everything associated with dishonor, including my past behavior. This is precisely the reason I wrote *Cop Out*. Not only to tell the world about my past failures, but to speak about the failures and injustices of rogue officers everywhere.

When approached by a law enforcement officer, do as he commands until he has determined you are no threat to him. In most cases, especially if he's an honorable officer, you will have no problem. If he's rogue, it doesn't matter what you do, he will attempt to violate your rights anyway. If you encounter such officers, know how to handle the situation. Read my other articles on this subject to protect yourself.

Obey all laws and take care of yourself.

Bad Cops and Seat Belt Laws

What's the relationship between bad cops and seat belt laws? No, I'm not about to suggest seat belt laws are bad. In fact, seat belts have been proven to save many lives. So what's the relationship between the two? Not wearing a seat belt gives a rogue or bad cop the probable cause to stop you and abuse his power. Remember, a rogue cop will fabricate any reason to stop you, but at least you shouldn't give him the *right* to stop you.

Many police departments across the country are now passing budget proposals to install on-board cameras in police vehicles. This is a good idea! It protects you and the officer with a tape of the events leading up to the stop. Of course, this is awful for a rogue cop. He needs and depends on stealth and privacy. He doesn't want any evidence concerning his possible bad stop.

By law, no driver can be stopped without a clear violation of some law. The only case is when a police roadblock is established to check *all* vehicles for any violations.

And while we're talking about cops, this article is pertaining only to bad cops. A decent cop is not going to stop you without probable cause. A rogue cop will stop you for any reason.

Do yourself a favor and wear your seat belt. I know it's difficult and cumbersome to wear one. I struggle with this every time I enter my vehicle. But I believe one can develop the habit of clicking the belt. If you need a motive other than safety, think about that bad cop.

Drive safe, obey all laws, and arrive home safely.

COMMENTS FROM DR. DAVIDSON

Safety is a basic need of human beings. Wearing seat belts have been proven to save lives. Some may dispute the comfortableness of seat belts, while others applaud these restraining devices. Entering a vehicle without clicking the seat belt is taking a dangerous risk. An individual may endanger his/her life as well as the lives of others by neglecting this safety device.

Risk takers crave the rush they believe occurs during perilous encounters. Yet, it remains to be seen the roads are no place for those who desire blasts of endorphins flowing in the brain. Physical activity or exercise is the safer (and less hazardous) way to create a similar effect.

Bad Cops in Grand Rapids, Michigan?

Are cops who have sex on the job bad cops? Paulette C. from the area of Grand Rapids, Michigan provided some information about cops having sex on the job with other cops or staff and asked if these cops are rogue. Apparently, there is a case in the Grand Rapids, Michigan area that has a lot of people upset.

Before answering this question, I spoke with a police officer I knew in that area to get more detailed information about the case and probed via the internet. My research turned up more than the reader provided. Specifically, the allegation that six cops were having sexual intercourse with a police dispatcher *inside* the police station! The dispatcher's name was mentioned and the officers' names were mentioned in the city's newspaper. Three of the officers were suspended and at the time, I don't know the status of the other officers.

My answer ... a rogue cop is a cop that violates the rights of other citizens through intimidation, duress, or violence. These cops are not rogue by definition. Any police officer taking the chance and liberty to have sex in a police station is pretty bold though! Six officers having sexual contact in the same station is almost unbelievable!

I wrote in my memoir that while an officer years ago, I observed similar acts. During my tenure, it was common on the force. I hope those kinds of acts are no longer tolerated. At the very least, it causes citizens concern that such actions are occurring within their tax supported facility.

COMMENTS FROM DR. DAVIDSON

The ethics involved with persons engaging in sexual activity on the job are serious. In the mental health profession, ethical codes prohibit sexual involvement with clients. On the other hand, these codes do not forbid sexual activity with colleagues. Although involvement in the workplace may be common, one's standards may discourage workplace romance.

Values are the moral fiber of human beings. Usually, one's moral principles were shaped by parents or guardians. Consequently, if people's cognitive processes are flawed, their emotional status and impending behavior develop habits that form faulty characters.

Certainly, sexual activity inside co-worker's offices, staff lounges, or restrooms are risky. Nevertheless, if one's character deems this activity as acceptable, then the person will make choices according to his/her ethical implications.

2

PREDATORS AND FUGITIVES

The Television Show "To Catch a Predator": Is It Entrapment?

I've been asked this question a number of times and after reviewing several segments, I feel I can give my opinion. Sheila A. inquired, "Is this show entrapping people or is it a legal and fair way for law enforcement to jail potential felons?"

Well let's look at the two sides. First, the side that says arrest them!

People that feel this way say the suspect is fully aware before hand he's visiting or speaking over the internet with a minor, a clear violation of the law. Furthermore, they say if the set up wasn't performed, this suspect would have violated a child. In my opinion, they make a good point (especially legally speaking).

The other side says he didn't actually carry out the crime. Sure, he might have known it was a minor and some will even say he might have committed the act without this intervention, but the act wasn't *actually* carried out. In other words, the crime wasn't committed. In my opinion, they make a good point also.

Here is the mode from a law enforcement standard. He actually broke the law when he entered the residence. First, probable cause (see my other articles on this subject) to arrest him was relevant initially when he spoke knowingly with a minor about sex. This is the point that hurts the perpetrator. It's not that he chats with a minor that hurts him; it's the sexually spoken content with a minor. If there were no sexual discussions, there is no intent to commit a crime. At least not clear intent of a sexual crime. Subsequently, my answer is the arrest is valid based on the law.

With that said, here is my problem. It is the arrest of the few who arrived at the house, parked for a few minutes, and then left. Can't a person have original intent but change their mind? Is it really necessary to arrest him? In other words, can he be given the chance to repent? I'm not speaking of the ones that while driving up to the residence observed an officer arresting a subject and then fled or a subject who senses something is wrong and feels he might be set up. I'm speaking about true repentance. How many of you have thought of committing a crime but didn't carry it out because of remorse, fear of jail, or for whatever reason?

Yes, the ones that entered the residences broke the law. But I'm willing to keep an open mind about the ones who are repentant. We are no saints. A sin is a sin. There are no great ones, but according to the law this is not quite the truth. The law differentiates crimes. This is precisely the reason a murder charge will always be viewed much more seriously than a manslaughter charge, even though both involve the taking of a human life.

What is the best policy? Avoid speaking sexually on the internet with *anyone*. You don't know who you're speaking with anyway.

COMMENTS FROM DR. DAVIDSON

Predators have psychological issues ... perhaps, some unmet need as a child or the lack of love from a parent. Whatever the cause, predators should be punished in order to prevent the potential ruining of the next generation. Entrapment is just a means to capture the criminal mind before one engages in the infraction. Whether the predators actually entered the residence or sat in their vehicle, the cognitive processes were still intent on obtaining their reward through the demise of a youth.

The predator has one goal in mind, to prey on unsuspecting victims. These individuals must be assisted with therapeutic interventions to determine the root of their problems. The next generation is counting on it!

Fugitives and Extraditions

Recently, I was interviewed by Paula Todd, host of Canada's national show called *The Verdict*. It's a crime talk show that examines the issues of current major crimes and court cases. The show is televised throughout the country of Canada as well as portions of the United States.

I was invited to join a discussion panel with others about Jesse Imeson, the accused murderer and fugitive from Canada, where a major manhunt is currently taking place. He was alleged to have murdered three people. My comments and opinions were solicited as I was a former fugitive for 22 years, with much of that time evading law enforcement by hiding in woods and forests. It's believed the suspect could possibly be thinking of attempting to hide out in wooded terrain.

This article was important for me to write as it also involved something many people asked me to discuss: extraditions.

Extradition is the act of a state or country requesting a person be returned to the original venue where a crime supposedly took place. In essence, the authorities are accusing you of committing a crime in their jurisdiction. They are requesting your return to face the charges (extradited) and if found guilty to serve prison time.

The process is basically an identification hearing. A hearing is held by a federal judge to determine if you are that person. That's it! Are you *that* person? The judge doesn't hear any evidence concerning the crime you are alleged to have committed. The judge's job is to establish identity. Once established, you are extradited.

Are there any exceptions one might not be returned? Yes, generally three.

1. You can prove you are not that person.

2. You can prove you were not in the country or state at the time the crime occurred.

3. The country requesting extradition doesn't have a treaty with the United States.

Yes, extraditions between countries are agreed upon through signed treaties. If there is no treaty, the country has no obligation to honor the request. In fact, there are some countries that have no extradition treaty with the United States.

I hope this describes the basic dynamics of extradition proceedings.

COMMENTS FROM DR. DAVIDSON

Intense panic might contribute to the desertion by persons committing a crime. The anxiety associated with impending arrest and incarceration may cause the perpetrator to flee without consideration of family, friends, or occupation.

The fugitive may believe he/she will be given unfair treatment if prosecuted or may die in prison. Some might fear retribution from the victim's loved ones. Yet, the decision to abandon all has precedence over any emotional attachment or professional goals one might have achieved.

Fear is a strong emotion. One must overcome this emotion through revising the cognitive process contributing to this dread or worry with the assistance of a mental health professional. If successful, fear might not lead a person to make inappropriate choices, but to conquer the issue directly.

3

CORRUPTION

Corruption and the Human Element

Why do some people gravitate more towards corruption than honesty? Darlene P. asked me this question the other day and what a question! Corruption is the evil human element that took me down 28 years ago. It is the element that caused my once promising career to end in disgrace, along with the termination of a young marriage and the loss of raising a son.

I often wonder where my life might be at this time if I hadn't made certain choices years ago. The zeal I possessed as a young police officer leaves me no doubt I would have become the police chief or other leading officer. I had zeal, but it wasn't properly guided.

Corruption is a choice. It's a choice we all make as we live this human life. Why is it some choose honesty and some choose corruption? The short answer is greed. I've learned through the years many things that can be stolen or taken through greed are attainable through legal means. But the corrupt person is only interested in short cuts. They want it now.

On the other hand, honesty is usually taught and accepted as youths. Usually, it involves loving parent(s) and in many cases a loving extended family. In many cases, honest people can't understand the vain decisions of corrupt people. In the meantime, the people who easily choose corruption can't fathom waiting for anything that's accessible at the moment.

When an honest person chooses to wait for something instead of stealing, lying, or receiving it through illegal means, he can never get in trouble. But a corrupt person can assure themselves trouble is on the way. In essence, the decisions are all about now (in the present) with corrupt individuals.

I am thankful for all my readers and supporters these last few years. I appreciate many of you who accepted my apologies and/or understand my attempts to "do the right thing" now. I'm not perfect, but I'm certainly wiser. Currently, I have the power to say I'm sorry and make amends. Sure, I know there will be a few who will never acknowledge my request for forgiveness for the past, but the fact that most accept my apologies is good enough for me. However, I will work extremely hard to win them over through my writings and dedication to expose all bad law enforcers. No cop or any human has the right to violate anyone—ever!

One of the Most Corrupt Cities in the United States … New Orleans

Recently, I was listening to a radio program broadcasted from New Orleans, Louisiana on or about October 9, 2007 that reported New

Orleans was listed as the most corrupt city in the United States (WWL radio in New Orleans). Many of my supporters and readers heard this announcement and commented about the assertions written in my book called *Cop Out* regarding this same problem.

In my book, I recount the climate of affairs within the New Orleans Police Department as of 1979. Namely, that the police department was a corrupt agency. In many of my interviews, I also speak about the political atmosphere and climate of affairs with other political officials in this city.

This statement on the radio was also reported on several other television programs and networks that same day. Quite frankly, they sounded surprised. Not me! I'm sure others that know Louisiana (particularly residents of New Orleans) were not surprised either.

As this information was reported, I was heading to New Orleans due to some business that brought me into various city offices for a few days. I spoke with many of the native residents who were aware of the fact I am an author including my assertions that New Orleans is a corrupt city. Many of the city employees congratulated me and asked me to continue to expose the city's corruption during my interviews and speeches. I promised them to do just that.

As I visited some of the city's public offices I was appalled. Many of the city workers (not all) speak to citizens like trash! Even if one visits some of the department stores and groceries, one can see the corruption.

I was truly saddened during my stop at the Orleans Parish Criminal District Court building located on Tulane Avenue and Broad Street. As you enter the building, some of the deputies in these courts treat you like dirt! In the meantime, as he/she is speaking offensively to the general public, he/she is speaking with respect to the attorneys or other important persons entering the same facility. And speaking of the court rooms, my guests informed me many of the judges expect to be treated like gods! They were right. As I toured some of the court rooms, I saw and felt the arrogant behaviors exuding from some of these men (at least the four I observed). I only witnessed one that treated you with respect.

If you enter a court room in Orleans Parish, anticipate a rude awakening. Expect to be treated and seated in certain areas like cattle. Moreover, you must speak and respond when they tell you. It goes way beyond being respectful to a judge or respecting the rule of law or the courts. It borders on pure corruption or a mass disrespect to anyone other than a police officer, attorney, elected official or other important person (oh ... by the way, if you're a friend of some of the deputies, sit where you like). Some secretaries, stenographers, clerks, and even janitors look at you with disdain and mistrust.

As I walked down the outside corridors of the courts, I observed police officers milling about and speaking crudely against the arrestees as they come to testify (even if the arrestee is there on a simple traffic violation). As you enter the court building, the deputies on duty rule. He (or she) will make sure you understand that he (or she) is the law. I saw many elderly citizens spoken to with no respect as they went through the metal detectors.

Almost everything in New Orleans is based on levels of importance, perceived wealth or power, or "what can you do for me?"

As I exited the various facilities with my guests, I was literally ill. My guests (also native New Orleanians) felt my disgust, but only after I pointed it out repeatedly. They mentioned the corruption is easy to get used to if you're there on a daily basis.

How can anyone be surprised about corruption in New Orleans? I was born in New Orleans and have never known the city not corrupt!

One of my readers asked, why the corruption? (Oh, the city is also known as one of the murder capitals of the United States).

Here is my opinion. New Orleans is a unique city. There are Blacks, Whites, French, and Spanish. Then, you have Blacks that are mixed with White called Creoles, Whites mixed with French called Cajuns, and so on. What is my angle? Simple … a power struggle has taken place over many years between the various races, sub-races, and mini races. It's never stopped.

People in this city have fought for positions all their lives and know nothing else. Everything that is of any importance in this city is fought over. Many have forgotten that whatever race you see yourself, we are still all one people!

Listen, I'm a native New Orleanian and want the best for my city and its residents. Several of my relatives still reside in the city. But as I revealed in my book, New Orleans is a sad and corrupt city. In my opinion, you might be more inclined to be violated by a police officer than a crook.

Remember, this city introduced one of the first police serial/spree killers, a female officer no less (Google Antoinette Franks), and a police officer who performed "hits" on citizens who got in his way (Google Len Davis). A disclaimer … both ex-officers claim their innocence and have appeals under way. Let's keep this in mind, arrest of police officers are occurring quite regularly in New Orleans.

As an ex-cop from New Orleans, I know for a certainty many of these officers got caught up in the corruption struggle. When I was on the force, I observed good officers fresh out of the academy "turned" in a few months by bad officers. I often wondered if Antoinette Franks and Len Davis got "turned".

Basically, the people in New Orleans are good people like many citizens in the United States. However, lots of them have been misguided and caught up in a unique situation that many in the world and in New Orleans are just learning about.

My final assessment … enjoy your visit to the city, but know it's not paradise.

A tip … when a city or state worker, court official, or anyone else treats you with disrespect, complain vigorously to someone in management. At least do your part to expose the corruption.

I'm saddened to have once been a part of this vanity, arrogance, and false respect, but now I am extremely delighted to be a part of a selected few who have dedicated their lives to exposing this foolishness.

COMMENTS FROM DR. DAVIDSON

Corruption is a wicked enemy of any political system. Whether occurring at the local, state, or national level, any form of dishonesty wrecks the foundation of the government system organized to protect the citizens it serves.

Employment in a facility where apparent corruption is prevalent may cause one to present unpleasant dispositions toward others outside of the organization. These negative attitudes may come from a root of bitterness directed toward the public, but most likely occur as a means of protection from individuals who are hurting. Daily exposure to life's problems might affect government personnel in various ways depending upon whom they serve—man or God.

4

SEARCHES AND SEIZURES

When Can the Police Search Your Home?

Today, we will explore the question about your rights within your dwelling. The question—when can a law enforcer legally search your home or apartment?

The answer—normally, he can only search your place of habitat under two circumstances. First, if he has obtained a legal search warrant from a judge. Did you believe you knew that? Well, there are some qualifiers. Initially, the warrant must dictate what will be searched. For instance, the warrant may say only search the garage or a certain room, or a particular area of the home. If the warrant says the police officer can search the entire home, he can search anywhere he chooses, and believe me he will. Please keep this in mind, if anything illegal is discovered during the search that doesn't pertain to the warrant, he can still use it against you. You could fight it in court, but your chances of winning are slim.

The second circumstance (and this is the one that bothers me to no end) is if you give him permission! The reason I'm disturbed by this is the founding fathers of the constitution gave us the right to dwell in our homes free from harassment. These are what they called *our* rights! Why would you give me or anyone the right to search your home? Yes, one might say, "What do you have to hide?" Well, I say that's none of your business! It's one of your fundamental rights and you should protect it. When the police ask to search your home, most of the time they're looking for a fugitive, illegal contraband, or any other illegal activities. The law expects *you* to live by the law. Therefore make sure the *law* lives by the law. Refuse the officers entry into your home unless they have a search warrant. Oh, one more thing. If he performs an illegal search, you will win if you sue the agency.

As many of you know, I'm not trying to tell anyone to break the law. I'm a former cop who knew all the tricks of rogue cops. This is my way to pay back society for all the wrong I've done. I'm just a strong advocate for human rights. I also know many people do not know their rights, so let's just say I'm assisting them.

Can the Police Kick My Door In If He Smells Pot?

Sam L. inquired, "Can a police officer kick my door in if he smells 'pot' outside my closed door?"

Actually, I dealt with this problem in a previous article involving searches, but I'm happy to review it again.

First the short answer.... *no*! Why? The officer must get a search warrant if he suspects there is sizable amount of marijuana in a home that meets distribution violation laws. Notice I said a *sizable* amount. Why a sizable amount? No judge is going to sign a search warrant request on one joint or a couple of joints.

Secondly, the officer is not an expert in smelling narcotics outside a closed door. Besides, the smell could be originating from another apartment or location.

Thirdly, unlike cop movies or shows on television, it's extremely difficult in the real world to get a search warrant. Police officers must first approach the judge with justifiable cause. Judges are extremely careful about permitting law enforcement to enter any dwelling. It becomes a question of constitutional rights. Believe me, it's a tedious request.

In the real world, the police are very unlikely to enter your home under these conditions. It's a direct challenge to your basic constitutional rights—to dwell in your home without harassment.

COMMENTS FROM DR. DAVIDSON

The smell of marijuana emanating from one's residence may be grounds for search and seizure. However, the more important issue here is one's need to use illegal substances.

The desire to use drugs regularly is a sign of addiction. Dependence upon any substance is a threat to one's being as well as others close to the abuser. Whether one consumes a joint or more for recreation or medicinal purposes, the power of the craving may cause one to perform acts against self or society, possibly leading to legal problems involving the need for police to search the residence. In that instance, kicking in one's door should be of great concern and may actually be the first step towards help for the drug abuser.

5

CIVIL LIBERTIES AND ARRESTS

The Importance of Your Miranda Rights

What are your Miranda rights? When should you be advised of your rights?

A reader asked me the above question about Miranda rights. She informed me there is currently a murder trial taking place in her home state heavily involving the question of citizens' Miranda rights, specifically when those rights should be read to you.

Miranda rights are civil liberties the police must read to you advising you of your right to remain silent. They are read when a law enforcer suspects you of committing a crime.

Folks, if you read my other articles you know my feelings about this question. Namely, whenever a law enforcer (police, sheriffs, FBI agents, etc.) questions you extensively about anything, he or she probably suspects you of committing a crime, or at least you should consider he or she suspects you of committing a crime. I advise all citizens to simply *shut up*, ask for a legal representative, and let the attorney deal with your defense.

Most police interrogators will not advise you of your Miranda rights until *after* you have incriminated yourself (this is actually a violation of federal law, but you can't prove it).

Listen to this! Why would the police advise you of your rights *before* you start running your mouth? Why would he or she desire to help and assist a complete stranger? In many instances, don't you know police officers' careers and promotions are based on his or her arrest and apprehension records? Do you really think he wants to help you? Please!

He or she has a mortgage or rent, a car note, and other financial obligations, not to mention the possibility of caring for a spouse and/or children. My point … this is simply a job to him or her.

Please, don't wait on anyone to protect your constitutional rights or read your Miranda rights. Get an attorney, period!

What To Do When You Hear, You're Under Arrest

First, my primary advice to you is, *say nothing*. When you hear the words "you're under arrest", the police officer is no longer your advocate. In fact, the entire system is against you. The only advocate you have at this point is your attorney.

Frequently, I've watched various television shows like *Cops*, *Cold Case Files*, etc. and become so upset I can't see straight. Why? If you're placed under arrest, shut your mouth. If the officer asks you anything else, simply say you wish to see an attorney. By speaking, you will dig a deeper hole for your defense. The normal impulse is to defend yourself. However, this is not the time and surely not the person to attempt this with.

I'm not trying to be harsh, but *shut up*! The police officer will use this against you in court. As a matter of fact, anytime an officer questions you, you should be thinking quickly. Is he questioning me as a witness or as a potential perpetrator?

Be safe, obey the laws, and watch for my other articles about rogue police officers, their tactics, and unfair practices.

What To Do If You Are Under Arrest?

In this article, we will explore this serious event. I hope none of my readers are arrested, but if you are, here are a few good tips. As a matter of fact, here is my best tip. First, *shut your mouth*! Once you are advised you are placed under arrest, there is no need to say anything.

In fact, you could get yourself in deeper trouble. At this point, the officer is no longer your advocate. Actually, no one in the system will attempt to advocate your case. The only person that is your advocate at this point is your attorney.

Oftentimes, while I'm looking at television shows like *Cops, Cold Case Files*, etc., I become so upset with people talking too much as they are arrested. Just inform the police you do not wish to speak and you desire to see your lawyer. If they persist, keep repeating this. In fact, if questioned by an officer for any reason, you need to quickly assess if the officers' questioning is leaning towards implicating you or a prelude to an arrest. Read that statement again!

Actually, many people ask me for tips. Consequently, I insist they commit to an exercise. What's the exercise? Pretend *before* you are arrested, while you are free, how and what you will do if arrested.

Of course, I'm not telling some person to commit a crime, or even suggesting you might be detained by law enforcement. I am just saying prepare yourself just as you would prepare for any horrible event. We purchase automobile, death, disability, and other insurance in life all the time. So prepare to "purchase" insurance on an arrest! Besides, this is a threat to your well being. Sit down and think about it for a few minutes.

As a matter of fact, I suggest every time you see an officer giving a citation to someone, think about this exercise for a minute or two. I am not suggesting that you think about this continually, just occasionally.

By the way, don't speed, don't commit crimes, and arrive home safely.

COMMENTS FROM DR. DAVIDSON

The impulse to defend self is a naturally occurring emotion, generally leading to a corresponding action. The desire to reveal various spoken words in order to protect one's rights is a logical decision. The method used when disclosing innocence or guilt may determine whether law enforcement can establish a case against the individual.

Difficulties arise when the person reacts versus responds to the situation. Normally, a reaction is a sudden reply sometimes without cognitively preparing an answer directing the person's emotions. However, a response causes an individual to reflect before divulging information, probably leading to an appropriate reply. In other words, think before you speak!

If Arrested, How To Survive Safely in Jail Until You're Released

I was asked this question by a loyal reader. He assured me he was not planning to commit a crime. He only thought if he was ever arrested by a rogue cop or a couple of simple charges were placed against him and he had to go to jail, he wanted to know what to do or not to do until he made bond. That's a fair question.

First understand this—in a jail environment all social issues and norms don't apply. Literally, you are in what could be considered a dangerous environment. So, here are a few proven tips.

- Don't walk in jail trying to make friends.

- Don't introduce yourself or extend your hands to shake other inmates' hands.

- Don't ask an inmate for anything. This means don't ask for a cigarette, pencil or pen, food, nothing. Believe me, you'll pay back more than you borrowed. This could be in the form of sexual favors, etc.

- Don't stare at other prisoners.

- Don't be the first to say anything. Find a space or corner of the cell that no one has claimed and sit there.

Strategies to implement:

- Walk in as if you've been there before. Inmates will sense a first timer and try to intimidate you. They refer to this new inmate and his circumstances as "being in his first rodeo".

- If asked a question or if small talk is started by another prisoner, by all means converse, but only about that issue. This is also the perfect moment to say, "This is not my first rodeo." Inform them you've been in jail five times or more!

- Get most of your sleep during the daylight hours. Stay awake most of the night (most attempts of rapes occur late at night). The guards patrol more in the daylight.

- A follow-up to the last sentence. It's rare to be assaulted in a jail and much more common in a state prison. So don't worry excessively about assaults of this nature.

- Finally, be the inmate who rarely speaks, who's always daydreaming, or who's a little weird (i.e., talk to yourself if you must, *out loud*). Pace the floor. Inmates are usually afraid of someone who seems to have slight mental problems. They recognize this type of person may harm them.

Listen, I don't want anyone to become incarcerated, but if for some odd reason you find yourself in this predicament, think only about surviving.

When Can A Citizen Use Deadly Force?

Under what circumstances can a citizen use deadly force? This is a good question. A good friend asked me this tonight after reading my article about when the police can use deadly force.

Deadly force by anyone is the act of taking another's life when we believe our life is threatened. It is an act that a person feels is unavoidable. Actually, one's act to use deadly force is no different from the police officer's right to use deadly force.

Let's use an example. Suppose you're at home sleeping and someone breaks into your residence. As you awaken and approach this person, they demand you give them your valuables. They are in possession of a weapon (doesn't matter what kind) and says, "Give me your money or valuables or I will kill you." At this point, you manage somehow to get a weapon and kill them. This is justifiable homicide (a homicide is the act of taking a life). You felt your life was in danger and because of this emotion, you are justified to protect yourself.

Now, if they broke into your house with the intent of only stealing your property, and you knew this, you cannot use deadly force. Why? No life, including the criminal's life, is worth taking because of property. Property can be replaced, a life cannot. I know that sounds unfair, but that's the law (except in a few states such as Texas that have passed Castle laws).

Another example: Suppose a criminal breaks into your garage and you encounter the subject. You command him with a weapon to put up his hands and surrender. Then he attempts to run out the back door to escape and you shoot him in the back. In most states, you'll be arrested for murder. Why? The subject did not pose a threat to you or your person. In fact, I know of cases such as these that the criminal was able to successfully sue the owners of the property while still in prison for the burglary charge!

Deadly force is serious, whether committed by a police officer or a citizen.

Just remember this. If you know that your life is not under an immediate threat, don't shoot the subject. Just let them leave. But by all means, if you feel your life is at risk, do what you must!

Take care of yourself.

COMMENTS FROM DR. DAVIDSON

When using force in an apparent threatening situation, the individual makes a choice to protect self or harm another. Usually, the person chooses to protect self by any means necessary.

The threat of harm to one's physical body may cause emotionally charged behavior to occur, particularly if a perpetrator enters a residence with the intent to harm. The perpetrator should beware of an emotionally charged individual, especially when a person believes his/her life is at risk.

6

LEGAL IMPLICATIONS

What's the Difference Between Serial Killers and Spree Killers? Premeditated Murder or Manslaughter?

Martin R. asked me to clarify the difference between a serial killer and a spree killer. Pam L. queried, "What's the main difference between premeditated murder and manslaughter?"

Serial Killers:

A serial killer is a person who over some period of time murdered at least three people. Some will say at least two people. Quite often, it's more than three people. In numerous cases, the murders took place over a period of months or years. Examples are men like Ted Bundy, Jeffrey Dahmer or Henry Lee Lucas. Many times serial killers and their crimes are connected to rapes or sexual fantasies.

Spree Killers:

A spree killer usually murders his victims all within the same day or within a couple of days. Quite often, spree killers are set off by some type of emotional trigger. Around 1997, a guy named Andrew Cunanan murdered about five people within a couple of days, traveling from state to state. One of his final victims was a gentleman named Gianni Versace of the famous Versace family. Andrew Cunanan finally took his own life in Florida. He's a good example of a spree killer. Another example would be 19-year-old Robert Hawkins of Nebraska. In December 2007, he murdered eight people at the Von Maur store in Omaha, Nebraska before killing himself.

Premeditated Murder:

Premeditated murder is not only taking a life by another human being, but the major element that constitutes or completes the offense is a planned and methodical organization of the crime. In other words, a person is aware of what he is doing, plans the crime, and executes the plan.

Manslaughter:

Manslaughter is murder by another human being as well, but the major element or difference is what some states call "heat of passion". Heat of passion usually means the perpetrator is operating on complete emotion. It means they were incapable of using reason to understand neither the crime nor the repercussions of the penalties. In many instances, manslaughter is committed between people that know one another well.

I hope this explains the differences in a simple and easily understood way. Take care all, and remember to drive safely, obey all the laws, and arrive home safe.

COMMENTS FROM DR. DAVIDSON

Taking the life of another human being renounces the moral principles of society. Whether committing murder at selected intervals or in one setting or regardless if the crime is planned or sporadic, killing a person is the most sadistic and heinous act imaginable.

According to scripture, murder began with the first family and continues to permeate civilization today. Several motives such as emotional turmoil, bitterness, uncontrollable rage, jealousy, insanity and other vile behaviors have been studied. However, the perpetrator may be suffering from the lack of spiritual guidance. In some cases, the impulse and looming annihilation may be chemically induced via drugs and/or alcohol. In these instances, therapeutic intervention and/or spiritual counsel may aid the tormented soul.

What is Domestic Abuse?

Today, we will explore this growing and alarming problem called domestic abuse. First, domestic abuse is simply when anyone hits or attempts to harm you. It's not just related to couples, but can also be between two friends of the same sex or opposite sexes. In most cases though, it's between a man and a woman.

Many years ago as a police officer, I received countless dispatches to homes where a couple was fighting or arguing. In most of these cases, I requested that one of the parties leave the residence and return later when cooler heads might prevail.

Presently, you can get arrested easily for domestic violence. In today's world, lots of domestic violence calls can end up as homicides. Why? It's so easy for a couple to lose it. On top of that, everything that has been bugging the couple for months or even years is suddenly manifested through their altercations.

Currently, due to wisdom and age, I deduce that in several domestic arguments the couple is really dealing with old unresolved issues, not the issues that began these arguments. People argue about washing the dishes when the real problem is one of the parties feels used. Disputes about bills may occur, but the actual problem may be excessive frills.

It has always amazed me how two people can find love in the summer of June and find bitter hate in the winter of December.

The ultimate battle we should all want to win is the battle against domestic violence.

COMMENTS FROM DR. DAVIDSON

Domestic violence permeates society. The desire for control may cause one to violate their partner. Naturally, the rage is directed toward the person closest to the perpetrator. Physical abuse hurts both partners. If children witness these abusive encounters, they may model these actions creating a cycle of abuse in their lives. Therapeutic intervention may eliminate the cycle and bring about peaceful encounters within the family.

Usually, the root of domestic quarrels is fear. This apprehension may lead to the need for domination resulting in anger or rage. Fear overcomes the victim; harsh words may be exchanged and could lead to physical violence depending on the severity of the disagreement.

Anger is a natural response to an offensive situation. However, it must be properly channeled through intense communication and conflict resolution.

Tips to Avoid Rape

If I help one female avoid this crime … well my job was worth it. Here are some very good tips to avoid putting yourself in the position of becoming a victim of a sexual crime or robbery, theft, etc.

In your home:

- Use timers to regulate the lighting in your home, especially if you tend to work late.

- Place a pair of men's shoes, garments, or anything that might belong to a male outside your garage door, rear door, etc. if you live alone.

- Use *dog on premises* or *beware of dog* signs, and alarm decals on your doors, windows, etc.

- Use a generic message on your answering machine instead of your voice, preferably use a males' voice.

- Always peek quickly into your vehicle's rear seat when entering.

- During darkness, always have more lights on the outside of your residence than lights on inside your residence.

In the public:

- Never travel the same route to work or home. Change up at least three times weekly.

- Never valet park your vehicle. Someone could quickly make a duplicate of your keys.

- Use a locking gas cap. Someone could siphon your fuel at your job, home, etc. causing you to walk to seek assistance.

- Jog or exercise outdoors with at least a friend or pet.

- Walk around all street intersections alert and cautious.

- If grabbed, bite, scream, yell or do anything to get attention. Make sure you embed your nails into the assailants' skin. There may be a DNA match in the DNA data bank, leading to his identification.

What are Date Rape and its Elements?

A reader asked, "Is it rape or date rape?" This reader brought up an interesting question. They related that if a female agrees to have a sexual relationship with a male while on a date and just before the act is started (while the male is preparing to enter) then the female says no, but he continues with the act is that rape? The answer ... yes, that's rape.

Suppose he has already placed himself within her and then she says no. The answer ... it's a rape if he continues. If he stops, she cannot call anything up to that point rape.

What is *not* rape?

1. If she gives him permission or agrees to the act.

2. They both finished the act with her permission and then she claims rape after the act (usually done if the female has regrets about the act later).

The crime of rape is a very serious charge and/or allegation. In many ways it's difficult to prove. Also, it can be difficult to prove one did not commit the act. Most of the time, the two people are alone and in private.

The best policy for the male and female is not to go on dates unless you are fairly assured you know the person well enough that issues like these will not surface. This means the female should date a man with dignity and honor. Moreover, the male should date a lady that's not prone to making untrue accusations.

Dating should not end up with a crime allegation.

COMMENTS FROM DR. DAVIDSON

Persons contemplating or committing the act of sexual assault thrive on power and control of helpless individuals. The apparent "rush" the perpetrator obtains from this act brings a sense of well-being and empowerment to a person who is obviously suffering from insecurity.

Anyone who preys on another person while violating them in the most personal method imaginable (through penetration) feels the authority and power taken from the victim. Possibly due to acts being imposed upon them, the perpetrator may feel justified in this crime. Sexual assault is truly a serious violation upon any human being which must not be tolerated and certainly should not be a part of a casual dating experience.

What are the Elements that Constitute a Charge of Robbery?

This question was asked of me last night along with the elements of other crimes. I'll deal with this one now.

A robbery is when a person(s) demands a possession or article from another person(s) depriving the owner of possession or ownership. If you walk up to a person and demand their wallet or purse, that's a robbery. Suppose you don't have a weapon. It makes no difference, it's still a robbery. Let's presume you have a weapon. Then it's much more serious. It's now called aggravated robbery. What if you tell the victim you have a weapon but have none? It's still called aggravated robbery. Why? The victim believed you possessed a weapon.

Suppose you break into a home, demanded money from the victim(s) and then leave. It's aggravated robbery and a burglary (you unlawfully entered a dwelling).

Let's assume you demanded someone's vehicle or other conveyance. That's still a robbery along with possible theft charges (I'll deal with theft and burglary later).

Imagine you approached a person with a feather and gave the victim a piece of paper that read, "I want your money." The feather is so light it can't harm the victim. Also, you did not verbally demand money. What then? It's still an aggravated robbery. The elements that constitute the crime can be real or imagined! The point is the victim doesn't know your true intentions. You could poke him in the eye with the feather or maybe you can't speak. Either way, you're a goner!

Here's a piece of advice. Don't commit any crime and you don't need the definitions. Get the message?

What is a Burglary? What is Theft?

What are the elements that constitute a burglary? What about a theft charge?

Thomas H. and Fred G. will be happy to read this article. I promised them weeks ago I would discuss their questions. Okay, here we go.

If you break into someone's home or business, that is a burglary. Suppose you never took anything. It's still a burglary. Let's assume you break into a vehicle. It's still a burglary (i.e., a car is an extension of your home).

Suppose you broke into the vehicle, drove off, and later ditched the vehicle. That's a burglary and a theft. On the other hand, let's imagine a person left his automobile in the driveway with the keys in the ignition and the engine running. That's theft, not burglary. Here's a slight twist. If you had to break the glass, force the door open, or in any way use force to enter, that's burglary.

Burglary usually constitutes some type of force, no matter how slight. A theft can consist of force also, but in most cases it's involving taking or stealing something through no force without the owner's permission.

One reader raised this point, "Suppose I stole a garbage can sitting on the side of the curb." That's theft, not burglary. Then she followed with a good one. She asked, "Suppose I take a piece of paper out of the can." The answer is no crime has been committed. Why? The owners of the garbage can gave up any ownership of what was *inside* the garbage can long ago; they simply were using the can as an instrument to get rid of anything contained in it. They own the garbage can, not what it contains. Even if they inadvertently placed a diamond ring in the garbage can, it's still trash to the law. It's your gain and their loss.

This is the reason you should shred or destroy personal papers *before* placing them in a public area. It's fair game.

Finally, a challenge for my readers, "Can one stop someone else from rummaging in their garbage can if they saw this person?" (i.e., like searching for empty cans, bottles, etc.). I look forward to reading your responses.

COMMENTS FROM DR. DAVIDSON

Pilfering from others ruins the fiber of human beings. Both victim and perpetrator are damaged by this vile act. The victim may be injured physically or psychologically due to one's possessions being taken unwillingly. The psychological impact may be tremendous with lasting effects.

The perpetrator may be physically hurt by the victim or through an impending arrest. The mental and physical costs to both parties could be enormous. It's just not worth the risk.

What is a Clemency or Pardon?

Is it easy to receive a clemency or state pardon? This is a good question by a loyal reader.

A clemency is the act of completely removing one's criminal past. It's performed by the state in which the conviction was originally recorded, executed by the governor of that state. It's similar to a presidential pardon, but on a state level.

How difficult is it to receive one? You may be better off hitting the lottery! It's an extremely daunting task. It's a political decision, not a question of forgiveness. In theory, it's supposed to be based on the length of time the crime occurred and if the person requesting it has stayed crime free. In reality, it's something most governors won't touch.

Here is the reason along with an example:

Let's say forty years ago you were charged with a rape or murder (or any felony) at the age of 20. Since that time you've committed no crimes, lived a clean life, and in fact, wished you never committed the offense. You're now 60 years old, certainly much wiser. You served time forty years ago. Now you desire to open a small grocery store, but in order to sell beer you need a liquor license. In order to get the license, you must not have a felony record when they perform the background check. You surmise, "I'm going to apply for a clemency to get that crime removed." Therefore, you apply to the board and are granted a hearing (they will hear your case in most situations) and obtain your hearing date.

A few months later you're sitting before a hearing board (usually 3–5 people). You begin to explain your reasons for a clemency along with the fact this crime occurred a long time ago. After you're finished, guess what will happen? Members of that board will interrogate you to no end. One would have thought the crime happened two weeks ago. When they finish the interrogation, they will probably vote no (most cases are *no* votes). What might be the reason for the refusal?

The hearing board's vote is a recommendation to the governor. Do you think a sitting governor that may hold high aspirations for some other office is going to approve your request, especially when most governors run their campaigns on crime and punishment? No indeed!

As a matter of fact, I know of several sheriffs' deputies that viewed these proceedings and told me they don't know the reasons there are pardon or clemency hearings. Many have never seen a person granted a *yes* vote.

If numerous board members could speak to you privately they will say, don't even apply.

My suggestion: Open your store, just don't sell beer!

Please note: This article is not an opinion one way or the other as to whether this fictitious person and example should be given a clemency or not, or even if they deserved a clemency. I am simply explaining the dynamics of how most clemency boards operate!

COMMENTS FROM DR. DAVIDSON

Leniency from state officials is an act of compassion for persons who may have matured chronologically or holistically following some unlawful act. Obviously, the individual living a crime-free life has changed his/her thinking and behavior following the criminal act.

Perhaps, this individual received mental health counseling or a spiritual awakening. Recompense for transformation should be one of mercy and empathy. The ability to overcome a criminal past is a justifiable cause for benevolence towards an individual.

What's the Difference Between Probation and Parole?

A reader asked this noteworthy question. I'll try to give you the facts between the two.

First, parole is only given to an individual that is serving time in a penitentiary. If your original sentence is two years, it could be cut short by a year or so. Let's assume you served one year of a two-year sentence with no behavioral problems. Then you might go before the parole board and be eligible to serve your last year as a semi-free person. The reason I say semi-free is because you must serve that time crime-free. If you commit a violation or crime, you'll have to go back to prison and serve that last year, plus whatever sentence you received for the crime that put you back in the correctional facility!

Usually, probation is time given to a person in lieu of jail. Say you committed a crime that carries a sentence of two years. The judge could then suspend sending you to jail for two years and instruct you to serve that time a semi-free person. This means no criminal action must occur during those two years. If you commit a crime, off to jail you go for the original two years. It's typically given to people who committed a non-violent crime, have no criminal record, or if the judge simply has compassion for you.

Oh, before someone asks … what's a parole board? A parole board is a group of officials (usually consisting of 3–7 people) that reviews prisoners profiles to determine which are a risk to society and which might be trusted to faithfully perform the parole. They are frequently appointed by the governor of the state they represent.

I hope this explains the differences between the two actions. Take care all!

What's the Difference Between Civil and Criminal?

This is an excellent question. It's posed more than any other questions.

These are examples of criminal matters: Robberies, rapes, murders, thefts, burglaries, DUI's (driving under the influence), batteries, sex crimes, etc.

These are examples of civil matters: Repossession of any properties, garnishments, rental disputes, etc.

The best way to tell if a charge, allegation, or matter is civil or criminal in nature is to research the penalty. In other words, if the penalty can result in jail time, it's a criminal matter. If the penalty is a fine or loss of the subject at hand, that's civil.

Please keep this in mind though, in rare circumstances a civil matter can end up criminally.

An example: You purchase a vehicle, can no longer afford the car note, and a repossession order is placed on your vehicle. The "repo" man comes to take possession. As he begins to take your vehicle, you get into a physical struggle with him to prevent it. You hit him! Now you can be charged with battery. Your best defense in this kind of circumstance is to let him have the automobile. You can always purchase another vehicle. It's not worth it to go to jail and still lose your vehicle.

The Differences Between a Summons, Misdemeanor, and Felony Charge

If you have been following my articles, you know by now I write exclusively concerning altercations with police officers, stops by the police, or anything relating to law enforcement. What I would like to speak about now are charges levied against you by a law enforcement officer.

First, keep in mind an officers' charge against you is simply based on his perceptions of the events that have taken place. He based these facts on either what he observed or what he was told. His charge is not a fact. It's simply his or her perception of the events. Therefore, if you alleged you are innocent, that could very well be true. But don't try to defend yourself at that time. That's a decision made by a judge at a later date called your court date. As a result, do not attempt to argue your case with the officer. You will lose. Wait for your court date.

Now, let's start with a summons. A summons is simply a document you sign promising to appear before a judge on a given date. Take my word, whatever you did was not too serious. It's generally administered when it's involving domestic arguments, neighbors arguing, etc. Whatever the outcome in court, you have a 99.9% chance of going home that evening. As a matter of fact, when I was a police officer, I cannot remember one time a defendant was placed in jail on a summons.

With a misdemeanor, you could be placed under arrest. It's a charge a little more serious than a summons, with possible jail time or community service for one year or less. In some cases, you will have been arrested, stayed in jail one to five days (unless you made bond), appeared before a judge, and if found guilty, released on the time you've served (one to five days is common). If you are found innocent, you will still go home, but you lost a couple of days of your life. Maybe your accuser is placed in jail, or at the very least, they will be fined.

Felonies are a different ballgame. It's a crime that you could receive up to one year and one day or more (i.e., at least one day over a year). It's very serious. You could still be freed, but it depends on a number on things such as your prior arrests, times between arrests, number of times arrested, the severity of the existing felony charge, and many other variables. You could still beat the charge, but most of these types of charges require an attorney. Don't ever decide to defend yourself on a felony indictment. It's too complex, so don't gamble with your life.

Lastly, I must say this—you could meet up with a rogue officer and be charged with something you didn't do.

Drive safely, obey all laws, and arrive home to your family.

7

LIE DETECTORS AND RADAR DETECTORS

Should One Take a Lie Detector Test if Asked by the Police?

Are lie detector tests accurate? I was asked this question today by a reader who stated he's been requested to take the test. I answered the question privately, but after considerable thought, I decided to let all my readers know my answer. First, I will give the brief answer for those of you who wish to move on and read my other articles (smile). Then, I'll explain in detail my short answer to those of you who enjoy facts.

The answer, *no way period!*

Now, here is the explanation. If you're asked to take a lie detector test, you are already a suspect. Lie detector tests measure breathing, heart, and pulse rates to determine if you're lying (that's what they say). The theory is that a liar's physical changes will increase due to nervousness. Folks, anyone's physical measurements can change when under stress, especially if questioned by police officers under these circumstances.

Oddly, even if you're guilty of the crime you could still pass the examination by taking a few drugs that alter or relax the central nervous system, namely drugs like Valium®, Hydrocodone®, or Lorcet®. As a matter of fact, on enough Valium® one could tell the examiner you are a visitor from Pluto and pass the test!

Secondly, if you're not from Pluto, but a good liar from the planet Earth, you could pass the test easily by believing your lies!

Thirdly, *all* courts in the United States have ruled lie detector tests are inadmissible. Why? They are not reliable. A person could take the test Monday and pass, then fail on Tuesday!

So what is the reason the police ask you to take the test?

Their answer will be ... it's only a *tool* coupled with the investigation to *exclude* your participation in the crime. However, they neglect to mention if you fail the test, they will *include* you as a suspect! And please don't fall for the tricky mind question "if you're not guilty, why not clear yourself?" or "if you didn't commit the crime, what do you have to worry about?" Please, give me a break! The law dictates you must prove I committed the crime, not that I should prove it for you.

The real reason—they hope you don't know the test is unreliable and inadmissible in courts with the expectation that if you committed the crime, they will get a confession "on the spot." Just say no to the test, make them do their homework, and find the evidence to perform a proper investigation!

One might ask, Robert, why reveal this information to the public when real criminals can view it? Well, my first concern is for the innocent people who might not know the test is a waste of time and can send them through harassment and/or needless investigations by the police.

Even the Constitution of the United States (through very strong inferences and directives) says it's better to let the *guilty* be free, than to let one *innocent* person go to jail for a crime he didn't commit!

COMMENTS FROM DR. DAVIDSON

Deception, dishonesty, falsehood, untruth, fib, story, tall tale, propaganda, and misinformation all have the same meaning. Usually, the result of dishonesty is imminent exposure. Disclosure of these untruths may harm others and bring about trust issues. In a court room, perjury (lying under oath) has detrimental consequences.

Trickery in any form is wicked. The psyche of an individual whose purpose is to deceive others is flawed.

One probable cause of deception is fear. The ability to overcome fears may be managed through therapeutic intervention. However, through honesty, one should not experience anxiety with the prospect of undergoing lie detection devices.

Radar and Laser Detectors

Is it worth it to invest in a radar detector? What is a laser detector? What is a VG-2 device?

As many of you know, a radar detector allows a driver to know the police are nearby. It operates on wave bands or frequencies. There are primarily three bands: X, K, and Ka. X operates on 10.525 GHZ. K is a little higher at 24.150 GHZ, and the highest Ka operates at 33.400–36.000 GHZ. What is the reason there are three bands with more to follow? There is an electronic war going on between the police and radar producers!

When X bands were used by the police, radar companies produced X band detectors. Then the police went with a higher frequency device, namely K band. The war went on until the police finally "up the ante" by going laser. The laser focuses a narrow light beam. Actually, the correct term for laser is lidar, which stands for light detection and ranging.

The question, "is it worth it?" Perhaps it is worth it if you purchase a detector with both radar and laser capabilities. They tend to be much more expensive than standard radar detectors. They are worth it though! If you avoided a ticket, the unit pays for itself and with high insurance rates on the rise—well you understand.

What's a VG-2? It's a detector used by the police to detect your radar detector. Why? Some states have banned radar detectors. They don't want you to know they are lurking nearby. Read on!

Here's the truth. Those states that ban radar detectors are actually violating federal law! If you ever receive a ticket for having a radar detector, fight it in court. There is a little known law, obviously unknown to many states or ignored by states that gives you the right to own a detector. The law: The Communications Act of 1934. It guarantees any citizen the right to receive radio transmission on any frequency!

If you are driving through a state that doesn't allow it, simply purchase a detector that's capable of detecting a VG-2 unit nearby. Yes, the radar companies have done it again! There are now detectors that can detect *all* bands, including laser and VG-2. After your detector warns you of a VG-2 device nearby, simply take your detector off the dashboard.

My suggestion is to purchase the units made by Cobra®. They have dedicated their company to staying on top of cutting edge electronic devices. There may be others out there, but it's the one I investigated personally.

I'm not suggesting to anyone to break any speeding laws. I'm just simply advising any driver about the dynamics of radar and laser technology.

Drive safe, obey the laws, and arrive home safely!

8

POLICE AWARENESS

The FBI and the State Police: What Are Their Jurisdictional Powers?

What are the powers of the Federal Bureau of Investigation (FBI) and the State Police? Who are they? I will deal with these questions asked by Paula R.

The FBI: The FBI is a federally mandated law enforcement agency that is responsible for all crimes committed in the United States whether foreign or domestic. This means the agents employed by this organization have the power to arrest you for any crimes committed anywhere within the United States. I hope that's plain and clear. Yes, they can even cite you for traffic violations. Of course, they are not concerned about citations. Their primary focus is federal crimes. If you're committing a felony like money laundering, interstate stolen goods, massive drug dealing, weapons trading and selling, murders, kidnappings, bank robberies, and many other different federal crimes, they have jurisdiction to investigate and make arrests. This is the most powerful agency in the United States.

The State Police: This agency makes arrests within the assigned state. For example, the Illinois State Police can regulate and make an arrest anywhere within the State of Illinois. It doesn't matter what city in Illinois. Think of it as a city cop with state-wide powers. Typically, they patrol the interstate highways and the rural areas. As citizens we generally see them on the interstates. In addition, they are responsible for the personal protection of the Governor of that state. They are probably the one police agency we rarely come in contact with.

All law enforcement agencies are to be reckoned. Generally, it's simply a question of those officers' jurisdictional powers. Knowing the difference between a Sheriff, Constable, City Police, State Police, and FBI agent can help you understand what you're dealing with.

As you know, I don't advise anyone to break the law. My articles are primarily directed to the citizens to protect themselves against rogue cops. These officers don't care about the law, fairness, or legalities. They are only concerned about misuse of powers.

Drive safely and obey all laws.

What are the Differences Between a City Police Officer and a Sheriff?

A city police officer is commissioned to follow all laws within his jurisdiction. This means within the limits of the city. He cannot venture outside the city limits to arrest, stop, or question any person except under one circumstance. I'm glad you asked—he can go outside his jurisdiction if a crime or violation first occurred within his area and proceeded into another jurisdiction; it's called *hot pursuit* (please read my other article about jurisdiction). He is only authorized to perform his oath for that city's laws and ordinances. He cannot get involved with civil matters. He can only deal with criminal matters. Therefore, his powers are strictly limited.

A sheriff's officer or deputy is actually more powerful. It doesn't seem so, but it's true. The sheriffs' power extends throughout the entire county or as in Louisiana, the entire parish.

For instance, say you reside in Cook County, where Chicago is centered. A Chicago police officer can only enforce the laws in the city of Chicago, that is, within the city limits. But the Cook County Sheriff's Department can enforce the laws within Cook County. This may be outside the city limits of Chicago. He can also enforce the laws within Chicago's city limits. They have broad range. Usually, they perform civil matters such as evictions, warrants, and other civil issues. However, sheriffs often patrol outside the city limits. They have much more jurisdictional power than city police officers.

It's extremely rare to see a sheriff citing a driver for a traffic violation in the city. Also, it's even odder to observe a city cop issuing a citation outside the city limits.

Remember one thing, you shouldn't be violating the law within or outside the city limits. Nevertheless, I think it's important you know sheriffs are police officers also, with a much wider jurisdictional range.

How to Handle Many Police Situations When Stopped or Questioned

There are so many situations one could encounter regarding the police I couldn't possibly address all of them. However, I will attempt to answer this question in a general, generic, and abstract way.

Most encounters with a law enforcement officer are concerning some non-serious manner. Occasionally, it may be serious. But keep this in mind, a small and seemingly simple situation can escalate to something severe. This is the reason I advise anyone who is stopped or questioned by the police to take it seriously. This authority can wreck havoc in your life.

My first advice that many of my readers are familiar with is not to answer any questions or say anything when it's obviously a serious crime. Just shut up. The officer will surely attempt to play a mind game with you by stating, "If you have nothing to hide or if you're not guilty, why not talk to us?" Don't fall for this tactic!

Many times while looking at police stories or crime dramas, I become so upset I can't see straight. Several people have been placed in jail for voluntarily talking, even if they are innocent.

It is not your responsibility to help him convict you. It's not your job to prove your innocence. He must prove it. That's a constitutional requirement. Even if you're guilty, he (or rather the district attorney's office) must prove it. I'm not trying to help a guilty person get away with anything, but the law is clear—better to let one guilty person go, than convict one inno-cent person unfairly.

Now, when you're questioned by the police or have to engage him in any matter, always remember to speak softly and be courteous. Be firm, but remember, every comment you make will be used against you. I never understood the reasons they always said, "Your comments *can* and *will* be used against you in a court of law." Trust me folks, they *will* be used against you.

Furthermore, try not to give him anything voluntarily. If you decide to answer, only answer what you were asked. The only exception I can think of off the top of my head is if your voluntary statement is that of a witness to a crime. Then by all means assist the police. It's your civic duty. Just don't get caught up and get yourself in any trouble.

Here's the major rule and thought that should quickly enter your mind: Am I being questioned as a witness or as a potential suspect? The answer to this question should regulate how much you say or don't say. Always remember to protect yourself *first*!

Finally, when in doubt, *shut up*! If he has anything against you, he's going to arrest you anyway. Invoke your right to seek an attorney. He is your only true friend. The police are only your friend when you're in trou-ble, or called and sought his assistance, or any neutral situation he happens upon. If you're brought up on charges and the district attorney decides to prosecute you, you'll see. He will come at you with the full power and authority of the state.

Theoretically, the district attorney is supposed to be an advocate for you also if he believes you're innocent. But believe me, more times than not, if charges are dropped against you, it wasn't because they found you innocent. It was because they couldn't prove your guilt!

As many of you know, my mission in life is to expose all unfair law enforcement officers and their unfair tactics. Why? I was once a rogue officer myself. Through the years, I hated myself so much it literally made me sick. I also feel my eventual death may come from the hands of a rogue cop or law enforcer. He doesn't want me to reveal all his unfair tactics and procedures. But as I've already stated on many television shows, I don't care! I would rather die for something worthy than something worthless.

How to Always Defend Yourself Against the Police When Stopped

If you're like most citizens, you never think about being stopped by the police. Believe me, most of us get stopped whether you're rich or poor. The reason is because a police officer can't determine your status in the community until he stops you.

Sure, if you're driving a new Mercedes or Jaguar he might deduce you're not poor. However, in this day and age, he also knows the driver could have borrowed the vehicle or rented it. Besides, it's not the vehicle in violation most of the time, but the driver.

Always remember an officers' main advantage over you is your ignorance of the law. When an officer stops an attorney or anyone who is well acquainted with the law, he deals with this person differently than a regular citizen. He knows he could not only be fired, but put in jail. Trust me, every officer is leery concerning who they will be dealing with on traffic stops.

Below are a couple of key points to consider when approached by any law enforcement officer. Please keep in mind this is when dealing with honest officers. These points do not apply to a rogue officer. He'll do anything to violate the law in order to receive accolades, a pat on the back, or promotions. To deal with him, read my book called *Cop Out* and other articles I've written on this subject.

First, understand this, no officer can arrest you, search you or do anything to you without probable cause. This means an officer must have a reason most humans would agree with under those circumstances. He can't guess, presume or use theories to explain your actions. They must be reasons based on objectivity and a rational assumption.

In addition, he can't stop you just for driving down the highway. He can't even stop you because you may have swerved in a lane. Although if he observed you constantly swerving, it is *probable* cause you may be intoxicated. It's not conclusive proof, but enough that he may check it out. It's a constant and persistent action that leads one to think a law has been violated.

If he stops you and noticed slurred speech or an inability to stand, this action could propel him to investigate further through the use of a breath analyzer or any other test to establish your ability to drive.

All I'm saying is the police officer is not the law. He can only determine if you violated the law. He's a person just like you, except he has been given the authority to determine if a violation has occurred on the public streets. You were not given that authority.

So no matter if you are a driver or pedestrian, know your rights, obey the law, but by all means if you believe an officers' behavior is inappropriate, report it to the Internal Affairs Office. However, if you are stopped by an officer, show him respect just as you desire respect.

Drive safe, obey the laws, and arrive home safely.

Gestures that Might Avoid a Police Stop

This particular article could help you avoid a police stop. It may seem stupid or even ridiculous, but to an officer it says a lot. A police officer is constantly on the lookout for one thing: *out of the norm*. He's looking for events, drivers, pedestrians, and people that are out of place or out of the norm.

When I was a police officer and during conversations with fellow police officers, after major arrests or busts, we would share how stupid the driver or pedestrian acted prior to his/her capture. You see, in countless situations the perpetrator *helped* us make the arrest.

Here are a few examples: A sudden slow down in speed, an abrupt changing of lanes (especially a lane change to turn), an adjustment of the rearview mirror, suddenly rolling down the window (to air out the vehicle), constant head turning, and constant braking. All of these will get an officers' attention in a hurry. Well, since you may recognize these patterns, here are a few points to keep in mind while driving near a police unit.

First, be normal. Do not change whatever behavior you generally exhibit while driving. Second, drive as if the police unit is not there. In other words, concentrate on something else. Third, if you can't relax or concentrate, pull into a service station, a post office, a store, or any public place and resume driving later.

Now, here's my best. When I observed this behavior, I never stopped that vehicle. I hope I can explain this accurately. Place your right hand on the steering wheel (at the 12 o'clock position), take your left elbow and situate it on your door window sill, take your left hand and scratch your head, play with your hair, or if you're bald, rub your scalp. I can't explain it, but this action appears so normal and innocent it always caused me to look elsewhere. I believe it signals I'm not a criminal or violator.

I hope this article gives you a clue as to how simple gestures and movements might make a difference to a police officer.

As many of you know, my mission in life is to reveal unfair police tactics and procedures. But I also wish to help innocent drivers escape a confrontation with the police. Now, my only desire is to help the public.

Take care! Obey the laws and arrive home safely.

Can Police in One City Chase a Vehicle into Another City or Jurisdiction?

The other day I was asked this question by a loyal reader, "Why do you reveal the tactics of the police?" The answer is simple and twofold: First, police tactics and procedures are not secrets. They are taught in the academy, but most of these laws are common sense.

The second reason is (as most of you know) I was once a rogue officer and have devoted my life to revealing all unfair police tactics, with an emphasis on unfair. If an officer issues you a ticket or arrests you unjustly with full knowledge of his injustice, I wish to assist you in not only nullifying the citation or arrest, but to have that officer taken off the streets. Why? He's a threat to me, to you, and to your children. More importantly, if a cop takes these liberties he may graduate to bigger liberties. That's exactly what I did. I moved from smaller to larger incidents. It absolutely ruined my life. I lost a house, wife, family, and career. Moreover, I have no doubt I seriously affected the departments' image from a public affairs standpoint.

Now, since that's out the way, let me quit my raving and give you the answer to the original question regarding police chases. If you are speeding excessively or committed a felony while driving down the highway or local street in let's say Illinois, the police can pursue you to Indiana, Kentucky, Florida, over to Texas, up to Kansas, sideways to California and if possible China! If the police are in what they call "hot pursuit" it doesn't matter.

Of course, before he gets to China he would have called for other departments to join the chase, but the point is he can go wherever you go.

Before I close I would like to give this one tip. If stopped by a police car, pull over, take the ticket, and don't run. Guess what? In many cases an honorable and compassionate cop will simply give you a warning. Sorry folks, I've never seen or knew of a rogue cop giving warnings. I never did.

Should the Police Chase Vehicles and Risk Harm to the Public?

This question was posed by a concerned citizen. She asked this question very distressed about her family's welfare as they drive down the streets and highways. Since she asked my opinion about the subject, I was certainly in this position as an officer quite a few times in my career.

The answer is quite simple. If the chase is at high speeds—*no*! That's my humble opinion.

Killing another human being in an automobile accident is not worth it. In my opinion, even chasing a fleeing felon isn't worth killing another human. Chases should be disallowed—period. I can't think of a single instance where it might be valid. On the other hand, I must admit a slight reservation though in a special situation—if the chase is after a known serial killer or rapist.

Not surprisingly, many police chiefs are beginning to agree with me as they instruct their officers not to chase in several instances. The point is no human life is worth taking at any time. The police will probably catch up with him or her later anyway.

Now here's the twist. An officer *on the street* as this is going on tends to get caught up in the excitement of the chase. In other words, the officer is intent on catching the criminal—period. He's not thinking about the repercussion of the chase, only in the apprehension. His normal and calm reasoning gives over to his excited emotions.

During the chase, the officer is not even aware of the reason he is chasing the person. While I was in the police academy, chases were never covered in detail. We were not told *when* to chase, only *how* to chase.

Many innocent citizens and motorists have died as a result of police chases. Let's put more emphasis on saving a life than apprehending a fleeing motorist.

Can One Get Arrested for Speeding?

The answer to this question is yes. If you're speeding on a residential street that has a posted speed limit of 40 mph and you're doing 70 mph, or if speeding down an interstate highway with a posted limit of 70 mph and you're doing 100 mph, you will be arrested. The charge will be negligent operation of a vehicle (or that state's equivalent charge).

The law surmises you're driving so fast you will lose control and kill someone.

While on this subject, I'll ask all of you a question and give a reply later. Can a citizen be arrested for driving too slow?

Can one get arrested for driving too slow?

I enjoy answering the various questions readers submit via email. They are interesting to say the least. However, this one came to mind the other night. It's a great question.

Can a citizen be arrested for driving too slow? Yes. Why?

A citizen can be arrested for driving too slow for almost the same reasons as driving too fast, especially on an interstate highway, and particularly if the person insists on driving at a very slow speed. This is the key. Normally, the officer might warn him or give him a citation, but if he insists with this type of driving, he can be arrested. It's rare, but it can happen. This person may cause an accident faster than a speeder. They can upset the flow of traffic so bad an accident can happen quickly.

I know many of you answered no, but not so. This is a dangerous driver.

Imagine the posted speed limit is 55 mph and this person is doing 40 mph. Many drivers will have to brake excessively and/or change lanes rapidly. In addition, suppose this slow driver changes lanes at a slow speed. Instant chaos!

Personally, I never arrested a driver for slow speeds, but cited a driver for slow vehicle operation. He was doing 30 mph in a 55 mph zone. Vehicles were swerving all over the place. I spotted him in front of me at a distance of three quarters of a mile. It was about 10:00 am, normally a time of light traffic. This driver and his slow speed had traffic looking like rush hour. I hurriedly pulled this guy to the side to let traffic flow again. He was not an elderly person. In fact, he was a young driver. When I asked him about traveling too slow on an interstate highway he replied, "What's the problem?"

Anyway, to all you drivers, remember a driver's license is a privilege, not a right. Not only must you drive in a safe manner, but in a way that doesn't cause potential accidents or fatalities. This means speeding or driving too slow or anything disrupting the traffic situation.

Drive safe, obey good cops, report bad cops, and arrive home safely.

COMMENTS FROM DR. DAVIDSON

The risks associated with excessive speeding are tremendous. Persons driving at disproportionate speeds may cause harm to self and others. Traveling at irregular speeds might be stressful, especially during the rush hour.

The cost to the occupant(s), families, and the community are enormous. Moreover, (if arrested) legal issues abound with court costs imminent adding to the financial burden on the family. With rising expenses, the stress of impending financial ruin might bring about mental anguish and physical distress.

Driving is a privilege revered by those obtaining a license for the first time. The cost of driving hastily or at a snail's pace is not worth the risk to one's mental health and/or the body.

9

TICKETS AND DUI'S

Can You Successfully Defend a Ticket in Court Issued as a Result of Radar?

As soon as I replied to one article by a smart reader, another one comes to me. The question is, "Can you defend yourself in court against a radar device better than a cops' simple observation of your speed?" The answer is yes. In other words, the radar device has proven to be "out of calibration" sometimes. Also, you could make a case that the police unit's speedometer following you is out of calibration. By the way, you better use the exact words "out of calibration". Radar devices are known to be out of calibration by as much as 20 miles per hour. Wow!

Here's the dilemma, a typical traffic citation costs about $100.00. If you fight the ticket yourself and win—great. But take into consideration the time you spent coming back to court again. Will you lose money from your job in excess of the citation? Also, if you lose, you will pay the citation plus court costs. Now, I'm not stating you should pay an illegally issued citation, I'm just saying consider the costs. I notice most people will pay the ticket with no defense. But there are some people like me, who will dispute a $100.00 ticket harder than a chicken attempting to escape a fox. We fight on principle, not cost. We get a joy out of winning.

There is another reason besides increased insurance costs to fight a ticket. If driving is your occupation, then by all means fight it. Moreover, I hope you're not a principled person that happens to be a driver! All hell will break loose. You will tie the courts logs for years (ha-ha).

Seriously, consider the cost. If you were speeding, pay the ticket. If you were not speeding, you might still pay the ticket. One thing I must say—if the officer was a rogue cop, who falsely gave you a citation for doing 55 mph in a 20 mph zone, fight it. When you win, go to the Internal Affairs Department and report him. They will start checking up on his citation log. If you lose your case, still report him. You must get this cop off the street.

Two Simple Ways One Might Avoid a DWI or DUI Conviction

Recently, another loyal reader asked me an intriguing question. It's a question I thought about not because I didn't know the answer, but because of possible ethical issues. I emailed this individual and asked her the reason for her query. She replied, "I'm a student studying toxicology at a major university. My professor informed our class that no one can fool a breath analyzer test." Well, I decided to answer the question, but with the following disclaimer.

Drinking while driving is serious. You could kill or severely injure a fellow citizen. So don't drink and drive. As a matter of fact, don't violate the law at all!

Your professor is partially correct, but there is a way to avoid the actual conviction in court. The analyzer may be correct, but you might convince a judge the test was wrong. Sounds contradictory?

First, in most states the difference between a DWI and DUI are not the same. In the former, its involving alcohol, while in the latter, it's involving over the counter medications, prescriptions, or anything that will impair your ability to operate a vehicle. Some states call both DUI.

Now, let's deal with your professor. The simple spice called garlic could trick a test. Not a little, but a large amount. Certainly, it can reduce the total score on the analyzer.

Say for instance your state law caps a DWI at a score of 0.9. This means if your score is 0.8 or below, you're not legally intoxicated. A large amount of garlic consumed a few minutes before a test could bring your score down a few points. If you're driving at 0.9 and ate garlic just before the test, you could clock in at 0.7, which means you tricked it.

At this time, let's discuss the conviction part. If you were stopped in your vehicle and asked to take a test and you failed, you will be given a court date as well as a night or more in jail. When you bond out and appear in court, you could have a defense if you can prove the test was wrong. How? If you were taking any legal prescriptions containing alcohol or said you consumed something like … well, I can't mention that. But it's something easily available over the counter. My point is a judge has the power to rule based on intent. A DWI or DUI thrown out of court is not a conviction.

I must say this again. If you read any of my articles, you know I never suggest breaking the law. My focus is on those cops who violate the law.

I perceive this article as a debatable subject for the lady who asked the question. Now, she can go to class and debate her professor (smile). I learned life has very few absolutes. Most things have exceptions.

COMMENTS FROM DR. DAVIDSON

The law says drinking and driving are illegal. Driving a vehicle under the influence of alcohol or chemical substances may cause severe harm to others on the road and those within the vehicle. Persons getting behind the wheel of an automobile while inebriated pose a danger to society. Apparently, these people have no regard for their lives or others.

The potential risks involved with driving and drinking or using substances that impair one's judgment are not worth loss of life or the financial burden placed on families due to tragic accidents or lawsuits. Actually, this individual may need intervention from family members and/or friends to prohibit them from impaired driving. In most cases, therapeutic intervention will provide the tools needed to aid the abuser to live a sober and/or chemical-free life.

Ten Worst Speed Roadblocks and DUI Checkpoints in the Country

This article was researched personally by me and ten other current friends (police officers) to reveal the ten worst areas in the country for consistent roadblocks. A roadblock is when the police attempts to catch unsuspecting drivers with illegal contraband or speeding.

The ten police officers networked with other officers across the country to assist me with this project (we all belong to fraternities) and we could only cover the worst spots. I cannot give specific cities (legal issues) but only general areas in miles and directions from major cities. If you can't figure out the town with the information given, you probably shouldn't be driving.

The order is from number ten (bad) to number one (the worst—sure ticket or arrest). All mileage is exact. All locations are just off the *major* interstates or the closest major interstate (i.e., I-5, I-10, I-40, I-95, etc.) leaving the city.

10. 57 miles west of Boston

9. 45 miles east of San Diego

8. 15 miles west of Dallas

7. Exactly 23 miles west of Memphis

6. 17 miles west of Albany, NY

5. 52 miles east of Spokane

4. 26 miles north of New Orleans

3. 13 miles south of Cleveland

2. 56 miles west of Atlanta

1. 36–52 miles west of Jacksonville, Florida (AAA reported this site)

I am *not* providing this information to suggest speeding or drinking while driving. Mainly, it's for law abiding citizens who may wish to deviate from these hot spots or avoid getting caught up in these areas.

Increase Your Chances of Getting Out of a Traffic Ticket

You may have seen countless television shows about police involvement in the arrests of bank robbers, rapists, and participating in shootouts. However, most of a police officer's time is spent on traffic stops and domestic calls. This particular article will deal with traffic stops.

While a police officer, I probably stopped thousands of vehicles for various traffic violations, including stopping vehicles appearing suspicious. I will get straight to the point as to how to increase your chances of getting out of an impending ticket, as this allotted space is small.

First, pull over as soon as possible (i.e., as soon as you hear a siren or see the flashing lights). Why? Police officers are taught most drivers with guns or illegal contraband need time to dispose of them. You will greatly relax the officers' vocational and natural suspicions if done in this manner.

Next, try your best to get out of your vehicle before he gets out of his vehicle. But you must have your hands in plain view. Why? Police officers know a fugitive or criminal wants to put the police in an awkward position by having the officer approach his territory. Besides, most (if not all) criminals instinctively do not want to approach any situation if they are wrong. If ordered to get back into your vehicle, please comply.

Think of it like this. When you stole a cookie or anything from anybody, you would never seek out, be led to or want to be anywhere near the authority in question. This is a natural, humanistic behavior. As you approach the police vehicle, you will notice he will quickly exit his unit. This is good police training. He cannot be at a disadvantage.

Furthermore, (this is the most important point) voluntarily say to the officer you already know you are wrong. Do call him or her Sir or Ms., and be as cooperative as you can. When the officer asks for your insurance papers or registration papers, like most owners, they will be kept in your glove compartment. Ask politely, "Sir, the items are in my glove compartment, would you like to retrieve them?" This will assure the officer you have nothing to hide such as a weapon or illegal contraband. Most owners do not follow these rules. They are too consumed about their rights and dignity. A police officer has wide discretions. What difference does it make to succumb to his few minutes of power?

Get out of the ticket, arrive home safely, and keep your insurance rates low.

Does the Police Department Have Ticket Quotas?

In a previous article, you learned how to avoid traffic tickets when stopped by the police. If any of the readers wondered why I revealed so much information about how police officers operate, read my book. To those of you who are not privy to my book (available through Amazon, and Barnes and Noble Booksellers), here is a brief note.

I was a rogue police officer. I was a young arrogant cop seeking power instead of fairness. I am ashamed I dishonored the trust placed in my hands. Nevertheless, I must make sure other rogue cops do not violate the citizens as I did. Call it my gift to the world.

Now let's discuss the subject at hand. Are there quotas? In all major cities, the answer is no. The reason is that a police officers' salary is paid by that city's tax base. The major city collects taxes from many sources.

If it's a city with under 25,000 people, that is a different story. In small cities, the tax base is not large. Consequently, there is an unwritten understanding with the Chief of Police and the city council to increase revenue to the city through traffic tickets and fines. How else will the city raise revenues? At this point, unlike a large city, the police chief is placed under greater pressure to bring in funds. The chief becomes an instrument of politicians. The chief may not even realize he is being used.

For that reason, as you travel through major cities, don't worry. But if you travel through a small city or municipality, slow down. Besides, the police officers in these cities have nothing to do but look for out of town drivers. In major cities, they have numerous problems to tend to.

10

REFLECTIONS

Note: These reflections are articles I've written concerning how I felt about myself as a former rogue cop. I thought I should include these articles to let all readers of this book know of my current state of mind concerning my feelings about my earlier behavior. I have been asked many times about my former days as a police officer and have attempted to the best of my abilities to answer each question in an honest and straightforward manner. I am not proud of my past, but I'm certainly pleased with the fact I can own up to it.

How a Rogue Cop Repented: Heartfelt Words from a Former Rogue Cop

This article is about me and my law enforcement career. Today, I communicated via email with a reporter and anchor from a major news station in the metropolitan area where I reside. It brought me back to the late 70's, the time I became a rogue cop and dishonored the badge and the peoples' trust. He and I correspond often via email. Since my surrender as a twenty-two year fugitive, I frequently think about my past.

This friend, the news anchor, will be performing an interview with me to discuss details of my past life. He's an honorable and well-known person in my community. I watch his programs every evening and late nights. This man has no business interviewing or speaking to a man such as myself. He has honor. I have no honor.

Tonight, after reading his email, it brought tears to my eyes. Why? It's because he speaks to me with such high regard it hurts. I truly wish I had the dignity and respect he thinks I deserve. I am so sorry for all the wrongs in my past. I wish I had never been born. I don't want this shame, this pain, but I'm forced to live with it. Sure, I'm a free man now. I've written a book and created alliances with renowned individuals all over the United States, but something is missing.

After speaking with him I know now what it is: normality!

I'm only known now for the bad I've done. I'm recognized because I was rogue. The insane and horrible events in my past have made me appear special. I'm not special. I'm still ashamed. Even though what I did occurred 28 years ago, I still feel the cold, hard shame. His honor overshadows my dishonor to the point it sickens me.

I want to say this to all of you, try hard, extremely hard not to offend others and yourself. You will pay the price.

At this moment, I must get up, wipe these tears from my face, and attempt to appear respectable again.

Have I Received Threats for Revealing Tactics and Procedures of Rogue Cops?

I'm asked this question more than any other subject and I've answered it more than other inquiries. A few family members are concerned about my life. A reporter I know is always telling me to be safe.

Yes, I have received threats. However, I think I know when to notify the police or FBI. So far, I've had no problem. Most of the threats are through the "grapevine". They are the type of threats an individual says he heard from someone else. In criminal law, we call this hearsay!

I'm not worried because I know I'm doing the right thing. Hence, I'm okay.

Moreover, I was asked this question by a host of a television show a couple of weeks ago while on the air. I replied, "If I take a bullet for doing the right thing, that's the best way to die." Really, I'm not afraid to die!

What I'm doing now is bigger than me. It's a crusade. There are people like authors Stephen K. Peach and Mike Madigan who risked their personal lives for years. When I speak with them, I detect no worry, extreme caution, or fright in their voices. These men are dedicated to exposing all. By the way, read Stephen's book called *Friendly Fire? The Good, the Bad and the Corrupt* and Mike's book called *The Twisted Badge*. You'll be amazed.

I've been told by other authors that in their experiences, your worse enemies might come from a few family members and friends when you release a controversial book or attempt to tell the truth. Also, I've been told by many people to expect other people (known or unknown) from the past to make accusations and charges against me because I've written this type of book. I find some validity in the fact that people I wronged in the past or simply dated and didn't care about will attempt to castigate me. Moreover, I am aware that law enforcement officers or individuals in the system could attack me, attempt to frame me, quickly charge me with a bogus crime, or otherwise set me up.

My grandmother (the lady of my life) told me personally many times to *do the right thing*. Well, I'm heeding her advice. She went without many things in life to get me and my siblings to do right and not wrong.

In closing I will say this, I was a police officer long enough to know not only police tactics and procedures, but anyone's tactics and procedures. I observed everything while driving, walking, or shopping. I never leave or return to any location the same way. I'm just as alert today as when I patrolled the streets and dangerous places in New Orleans.

I believe I have just as good a chance to live a long life as most ordinary citizens because I know what to look for! While a fugitive, I depended on myself and no one else. It's funny … more people are concerned about me now than when I was destitute with no money, food or clothing. Some never cared and still don't care. Either way, I will survive by whatever means necessary.

About the Authors

Mr. Robert L. Davis is a former award winning police officer with the New Orleans Police Department. He studied criminal law at Loyola University. He is an avid outdoorsman and enjoys the rare sport of spelunking. He has dedicated his life to exposing bad cops.

Dr. Roxanne M. Davidson is an Associate Professor of Behavioral Studies at Southern University and A&M College in Baton Rouge, Louisiana. She is a Licensed Professional Counselor and a National Certified Counselor. Her areas of interest include social and cultural issues, marriage and family therapy, and clinical fieldwork.

978-0-595-48609-0
0-595-48609-6

www.ingramcontent.com/pod-product-compliance
Lightning Source LLC
Chambersburg PA
CBHW030347290526
45785CB00004B/1640